BUCKET BLAST

Songs and Activities for Schools
by Tom Anderson

MW00855767

TABLE OF CONTENTS

DIGITAL DOWNLOAD CODE
To access audio MP3 & instrumental PDF files, go to:
www.halleonard.com/mylibrary

4037-8954-4431-1364

TEACHER'S NOTE
Audio Recordings and
Instrumental PDFs are available
for Digital Download,
when these icons are present.

HAL•LEONARD®

Visit Hal Leonard Online at
www.halleonard.com

Contact us:
Hal Leonard
7777 West Bluemound Road
Milwaukee, WI 53213
Email: info@halleonard.com

In Europe, contact:
Hal Leonard Europe Limited
42 Wigmore Street
Marylebone, London, W1U 2RY
Email: info@halleonardeurope.com

In Australia, contact:
Hal Leonard Australia Pty. Ltd.
4 Lentara Court
Cheltenham, Victoria, 3192 Australia
Email: info@halleonard.com.au

INTRODUCTION TO BUCKET DRUMMING

Bucket drumming is fun. That is a given. But it can also be musical, promote teamwork, teach basic percussion technique, and lead to other musical activities like marching bands. So, let's begin.

25-LITRE PLASTIC BUCKET

Where to start? The obvious answer is to get a bucket. Most bucket drumming is done using a 25-litre plastic bucket, sometimes called a *tenor drum*.

It is placed on the ground with the bottom at the top. Remove the wire handle so it does not rattle. Most buckets can be purchased for less than £10, or you could get some donated. Of course, clean thoroughly before using.

WOODEN DRUMSTICKS

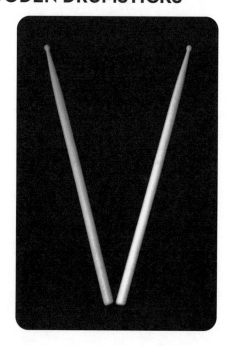

There are choices for what to use to strike the bucket. One solution is to purchase pairs of drumsticks (available for less than £5 in most music shops). It is recommended to use drumsticks with wood beads or tips so they will not possibly fly off like plastic-tip drumsticks.

One advantage of drumsticks is that they can be played using the tip, the middle called the *shoulder* and the fatter end called the *butt*. The more tones you can produce striking a bucket, the better. Wooden dowels can be used for playing bucket drums as well, or even rhythm sticks.

MATCHED GRIP

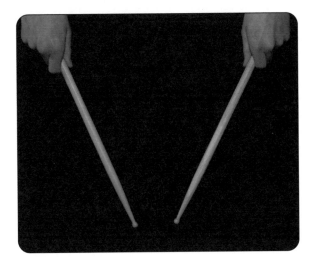

Bucket drumming uses the *matched grip* when holding the sticks. This is where the player holds each stick in the same way; much like you would hold a chicken drumstick at a picnic.

This grip is different than the *traditional grip* where the left stick is held between the middle and index fingers, commonly used by jazz and rudimentary drummers.

SITTING POSITION

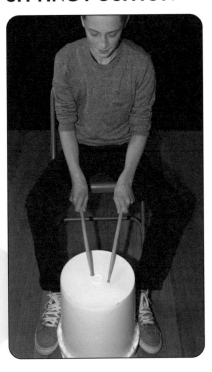

Bucket drummers can sit on anything that is convenient. When playing on street corners, they can even sit on another bucket. For our purposes, have them sit on a chair with their feet on both sides of the bucket. This is important because eventually they are going to tilt the buckets to produce a lower tone called a *bass tone*.

This resource features play-along activities for bucket drums and optional percussion. The recordings are rhythmic popular music from the past several decades.

There is a suggested warm-up that precedes each piece of music. These will help to prepare the players by introducing similar rhythms, techniques, and tones that are featured in each piece.

Now that everyone is in place, let's begin!

BUCKET DRUM NOTATION GUIDE

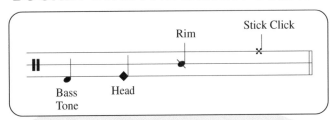

PLAY-ALONG WITH "ROCK AROUND THE CLOCK"

Teaching Tips by Tom Anderson

BUCKET DRUM WARM-UP 1

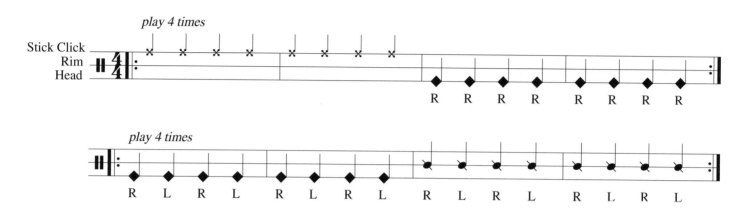

"Rock Around the Clock" by Bill Haley & His Comets is a great song to play for anything rhythmic. It starts with a distinctive rhythm that requires the players to keep track of when to play and when not to play. This rhythm is called *Stop Time*.

STICK CLICKS & BACK BEAT

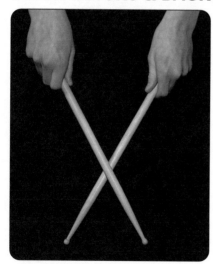

The first rhythm played by the bucket drummers does not even involve hitting the bucket. It is a series of stick clicks produced by hitting the middle of the sticks together.

The rhythm should match the accompaniment track where all of the instruments are playing at the same time.

The end of the Introduction is played on beats 2 and 4, called the *Back Beat*. This rhythm continues into the verse.

OPTIONAL PERCUSSION

Optional percussion parts are provided so that everyone can participate in the music-making. **Low drum** (like a bass drum) and **tambourine** are suggested for these parts. Point out that the low drum part is placed underneath the stave line, and the tambourine part is above the stave line. Pupils will need to watch for that when reading their separate instrument parts.

HEAD

The first bucket drum sound is produced by hitting in the middle of the bucket (or "head"). Use the tip of the stick when playing this tone.

The players can start by playing with one hand only. Eventually, they will need to be able to alternate their hands. This change is suggested in Warm-Up 1 where they play the first line using only the right hand (R), then alternating right and left (R) (L) in the second line.

RIM SHOT

The next tone to be played is produced by hitting the rim of the bucket and is called a *rim shot*. When done properly, this creates a "crack."

HEAD & RIM

The rhythm during the guitar solo alternates between hitting the bucket in the middle and hitting the bucket on the rim at the same time.

TEAMWORK, DYNAMICS, LISTENING

For variety, the bucket drummers can click their neighbours' sticks or their own sticks. Remember how bucket drumming can create teamwork? This cannot be done without the help of others.

Various dynamics are suggested. This is a great way to build musicianship and listening skills.

FINAL CHORD

All of the drums can be played with rolls and the tambourines can be shaken during the final chord. This is where alternating hands is an important technique to master. Bucket drummers can be future percussionists because many of their experiences can support future musical adventures.

PLAY-ALONG WITH "ROCK AROUND THE CLOCK"

Words and Music by MAX C. FREEDMAN
and JIMMY DeKNIGHT
Percussion Parts by TOM ANDERSON

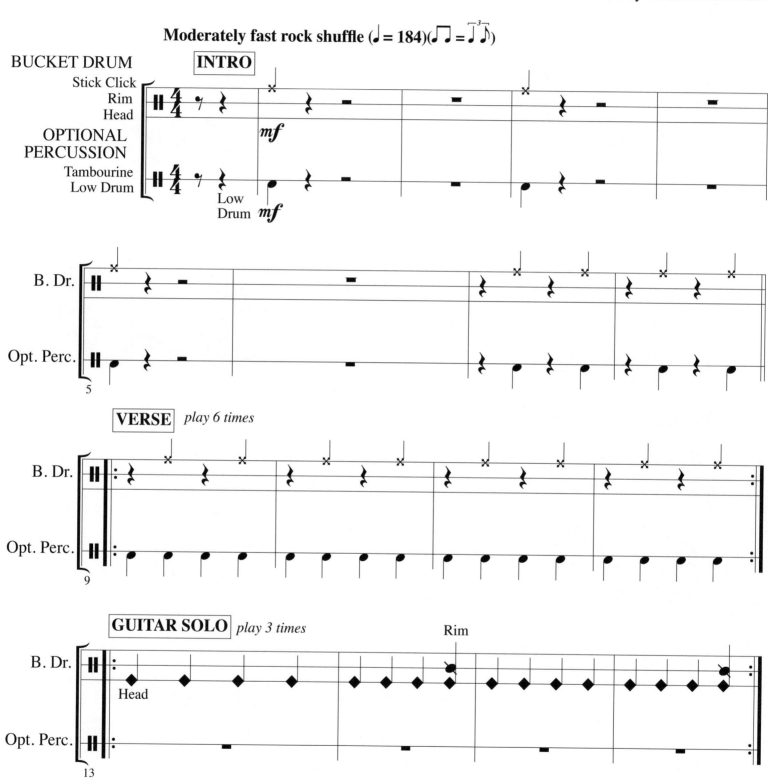

PLAY-ALONG WITH "SWEET HOME ALABAMA"

Teaching Tips by Tom Anderson

BUCKET DRUM WARM-UP 2

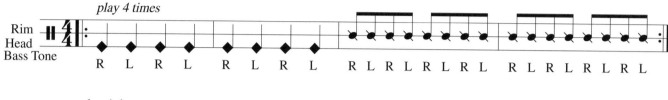

The opening guitar riff for "Sweet Home Alabama" by Lynyrd Skynyrd is instantly recognisable and makes you want to play along. The song features a steady rock beat that can be replicated on the bucket drum.

BASS TONE • RIM

A *bass tone* is played by tilting the bucket slightly with your foot. To add extra heft to the sound, use the fat end, or butt, of the stick; striking the bucket in the middle of the head.

A rock beat is created by playing two bass tones followed by hitting the rim. On a drum kit, this would be played on the bass drum and a *cross stick* (angled drumstick hitting the edge of the drum) on the snare drum.

HEAD · RIM

The other bucket drum rhythm involves playing the head, then the rim. This creates a "bam-clack-bam-clack" sound; a simple rock beat.

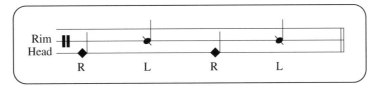

ADDITIONAL WARM-UPS

These two rhythms can be used to create various warm-ups. One warm-up would be to play the first rhythm four times followed by the second rhythm four times. Continue until the players are confident and not rushing the tempo.

Another warm-up is to have one group of bucket drummers play the first rhythm at the same time the other group plays the second. If they are doing it correctly, the rim hits will sound at the same time.

When the drummers know these two rhythms, they can play-along with the whole song!

OPTIONAL PERCUSSION

The optional percussion parts are **wood block** and **tambourine**. Those instruments are played using the same rhythm (on beats 2 and 4). It is a matter of keeping track of *when* they are to be played with the play-along track. If done properly, they sound at the same time as the rim hits of the bucket drums. Point out to pupils that the wood block part is notated above the stave line, and the tambourine part is below the stave line.

PLAY-ALONG WITH "SWEET HOME ALABAMA"

Words and Music by RONNIE VAN ZANT,
ED KING and GARY ROSSINGTON
Percussion Parts by TOM ANDERSON

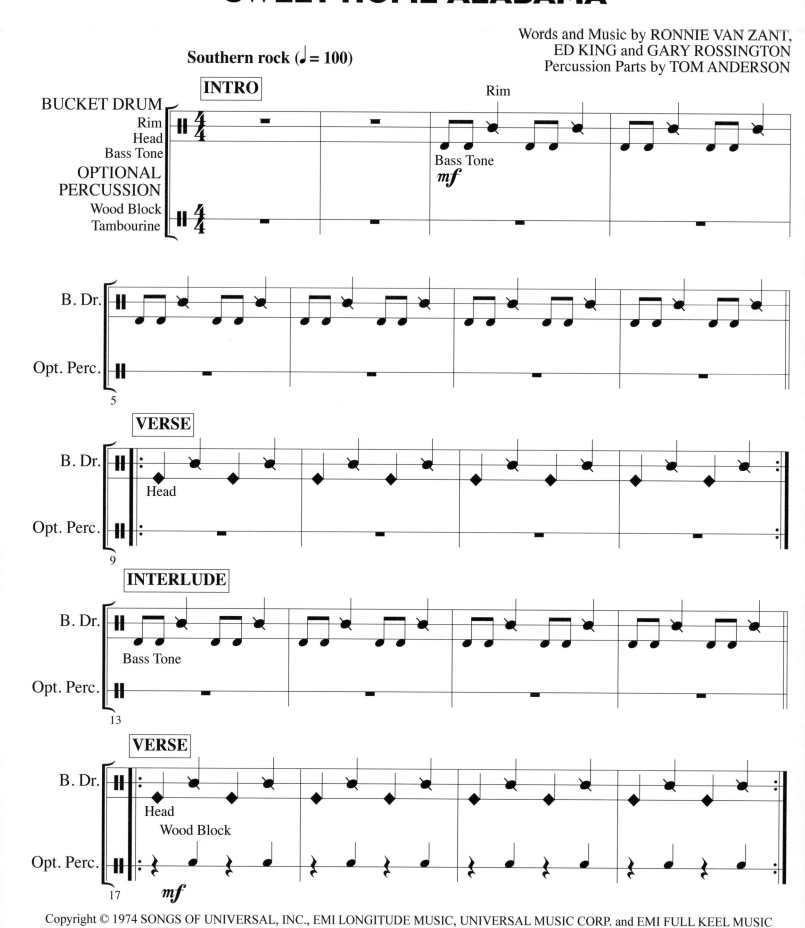

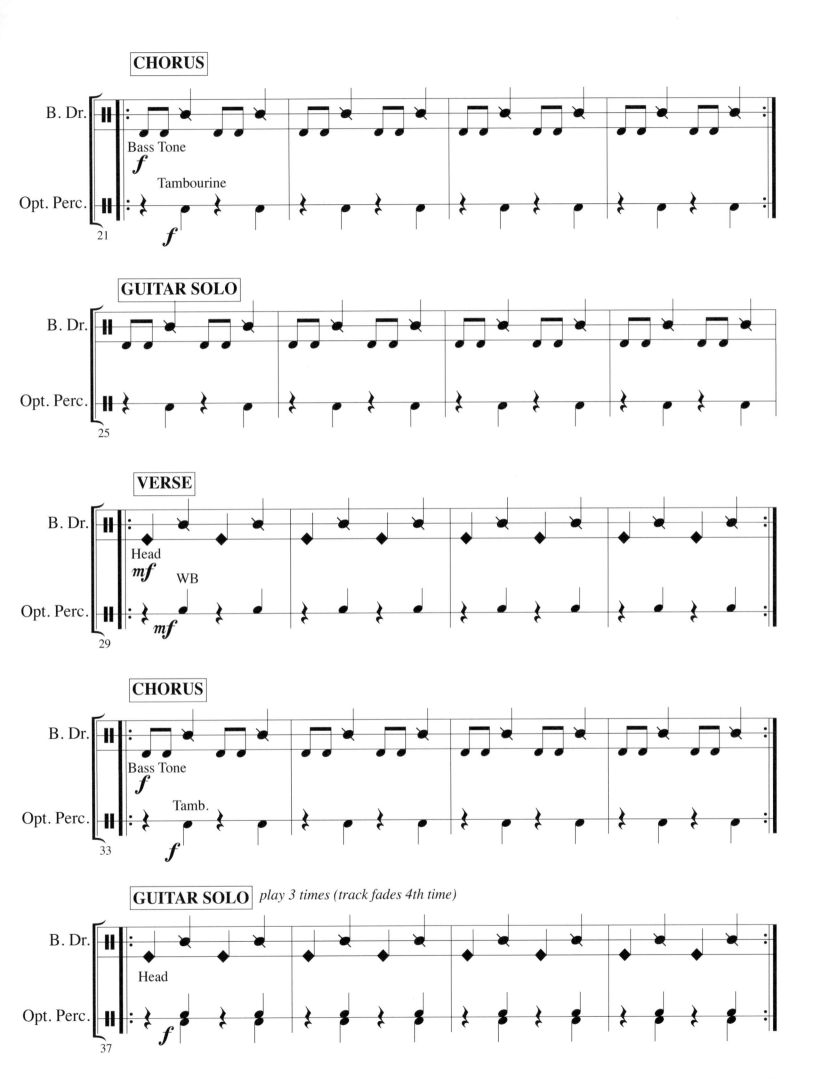

PLAY-ALONG WITH "I GOT YOU (I FEEL GOOD)"

Teaching Tips by Tom Anderson

BUCKET DRUM WARM-UP 3

"I Got You (I Feel Good)" by James Brown has an infectious groove that quickly established it as a Rhythm and Blues standard. The tight, funky rhythms combine with iconic sax licks to create a song made for dancing and music-making.

There are no new sounds to be played on the bucket drums, but now the sounds are combined. Warm-Up 3 includes playing the head and the rim at the same time, as well as a bass tone and rim. It is important to play these tones in sync with the sticks hitting at the same time. Also, each tone should be played with the same volume.

BASS TONE & RIM

The rock beat first played on the bucket drum features *syncopation* where a note falls on a "weak" beat or in between the beats. In this case, a bass tone is played on the "+" of beat 2 creating a rhythm similar to one played on a drum kit. The bass tone would be played on the bass drum and the rim hit would be played as a cross stick on the snare drum.

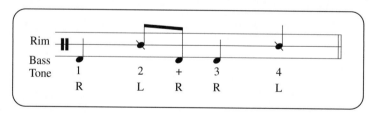

Repeat this rhythm until it is played with confidence and the tempo does not rush. Again, use the butt end of the stick to play the bass tone.

THE OFF BEAT

Another important rhythm in "I Got You (I Feel Good)" is to play on Beats 2 and 3 for two measures, followed by playing on the "+" of the beats (the *off beat*) five times. This rhythm matches the accompaniment. Again, work on synchronisation so that the sticks in both hands hit the bucket at the same time.

OPTIONAL PERCUSSION

The optional percussion parts are **wood block**, **hand claps**, and **tambourine**. Point out to the pupils where each part is notated on the stave. The tambourine is played mainly with quavers. Hold the instrument in the right hand so that it is vertical. Shake it back and forth in a steady motion left to right. Have it hit the left hand on the accented beats, 2 and 4.

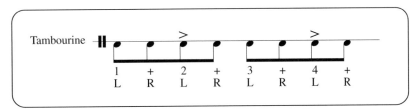

This quaver rhythm is often played (without the accents) on the ride cymbal or hi hat on a drum kit.

ROLL

A *roll* (rapidly moving your sticks) is played on the last, held note. This can be played as a *single-stroke roll* where each stick is hit once as quickly as possible. Play it in the middle of the bucket drum head.

PLAY-ALONG WITH
"I GOT YOU (I FEEL GOOD)"

Moderate R & B ($\quad$ = 144)

Words and Music by JAMES BROWN
Percussion Parts by TOM ANDERSON

BUCKET DRUM

Rim
Head
Bass Tone

OPTIONAL PERCUSSION

Wood Block
Hand Claps
Tambourine

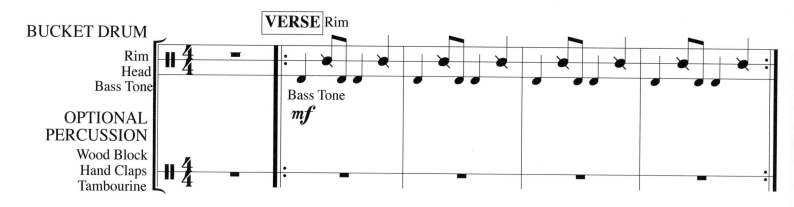

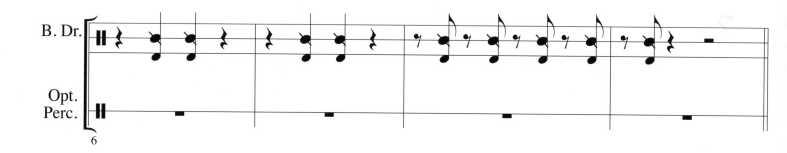

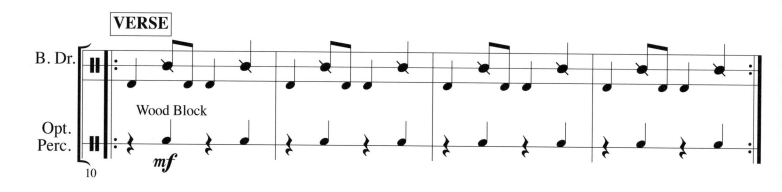

PLAY-ALONG WITH "SHAKE IT OFF"

Teaching Tips by Tom Anderson

BUCKET DRUM WARM-UP 4

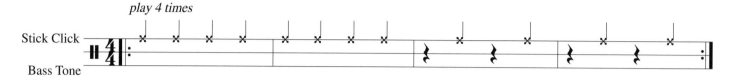

The lyrics for Taylor Swift's "Shake It Off" empower you to not worry about what other people think. The accompaniment is built over a bed of sounds directly from a marching band drumline. The original recording even features stick clicks!

The sounds and rhythms of the bucket drum part build on the previous arrangements. No new tones are introduced and many of the rhythms have already been played.

OFF BEAT STICK CLICKS

The first stick click rhythm is featured in Warm-Up 4; playing on the off beats. One helpful movement to reinforce this rhythm is to move your hands out on the rests and inward on beats 2 and 4.

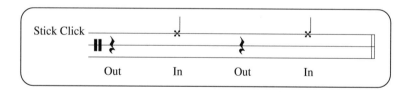

BASS TONE & RIM

The first rhythm played on the bucket drum begins with a rhythm that was featured in "I Got You (I Feel Good)" for one bar. This is followed by a bar of bass-rim-bass-rim forming a two-bar phrase.

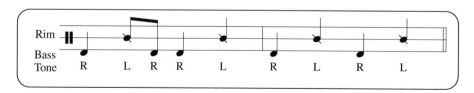

BREAKDOWN

There are two rhythms played during the *breakdown* section. Both rhythms are two bars in length.

OPTIONAL PERCUSSION

Hand claps are often on the off beats along with the stick clicks. Another rhythm is clapping on beat 2, the "+" of 2 and beat 4.

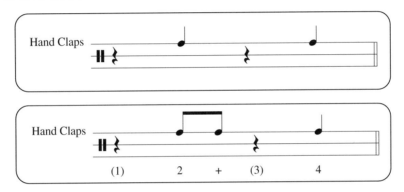

The **low drum** rhythm is similar to the first bucket drum breakdown rhythm. The only difference is the second bar is two minims instead of two crotchets.

The **shakers** rhythm alternates between playing crotchets and later quavers. Work for a crisp, clean sound when playing shakers by moving your hand quickly with short stops in between movements; much like a robotic motion. Allow the beads to hit the side of the shaker as opposed to swirling around the instrument.

Create an accent on beats 2 and 4 when playing quavers moving your hand slightly farther in front of you on those notes. Think, "One and TWO and Three and FOUR and."

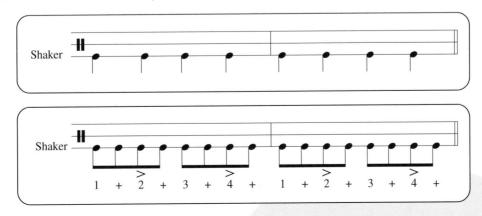

PLAY-ALONG WITH
"SHAKE IT OFF"

Words and Music by TAYLOR SWIFT,
MAX MARTIN and SHELLBACK
Percussion Parts by TOM ANDERSON

Fast dance groove (♩ = 149)

BUCKET DRUM

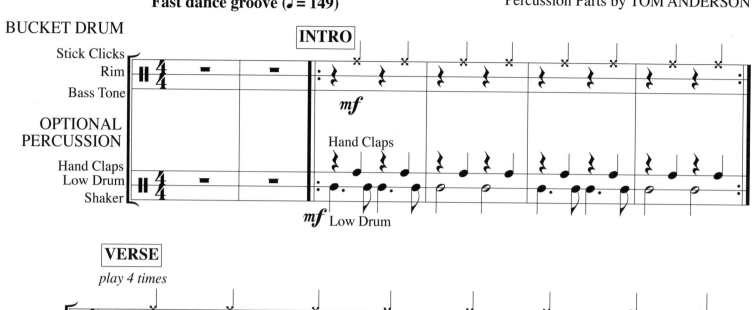

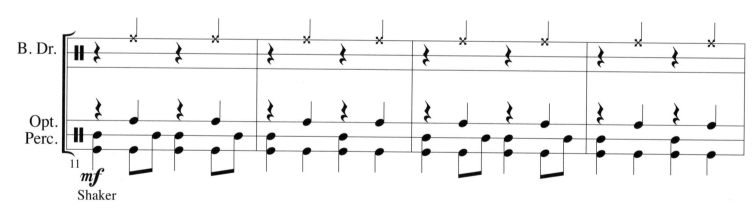

PLAY-ALONG WITH "FREE RIDE"

Teaching Tips by Tom Anderson

BUCKET DRUM WARM-UP 5

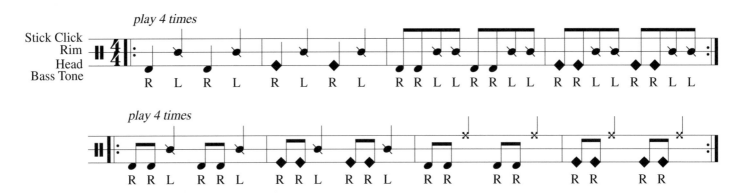

Now it is time to just have fun! "Free Ride" by The Edgar Winter Group continues its popularity by being featured on the radio, in films and adverts, as well as computer games. With its distinctive opening guitar riff and driving beat, this makes a perfect rock tune to jam along.

BASS TONE & RIM

The first bucket drum rhythm in the chorus is from Warm-Up 5. It is a quintessential rock beat played by drummers everywhere.

Sound familiar? It was played in "Sweet Home Alabama."

DRUM FILL

The most challenging bucket drum part is optional. It is a *fill* (a flourish of notes) played on the rim. It is the same rhythm as the guitar part with much syncopation. That is why it is optional.

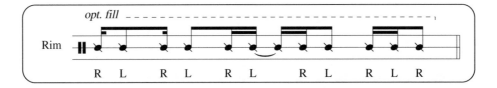

Even though it is fast, if you alternate your hands, it is playable. Lead with your "strong" hand. For most people, that is the right hand.

OPTIONAL PERCUSSION

The **tambourine** part alternates between quavers, crotchets, and playing on the off beats, 2 and 4.

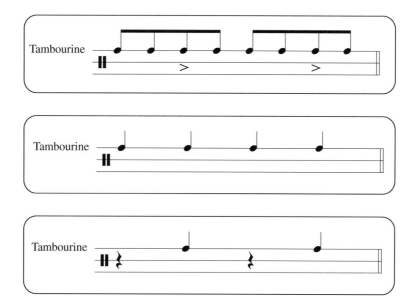

The music for the **cowbell** part looks deceptively simple, but it can be a challenge to play. The primary function of this part is to keep the beat, so **don't rush!**

Hold the cowbell so the *mouth* (the open end) is facing away from you. Wrap your fingers around it so that it doesn't ring freely. Hit the edge of the cowbell's mouth with the butt end of a drumstick. If done properly, it should produce a solid "clunk," "clunk," "clunk," "clunk" sound.

The **hand claps** begin on the off beats of 2 and 4, and then on all four beats in the bar.

PLAY-ALONG WITH
"FREE RIDE"

Moderate Rock ($\quarternote$ = 126)

Words and Music by DAN HARTMAN
Percussion Parts by TOM ANDERSON

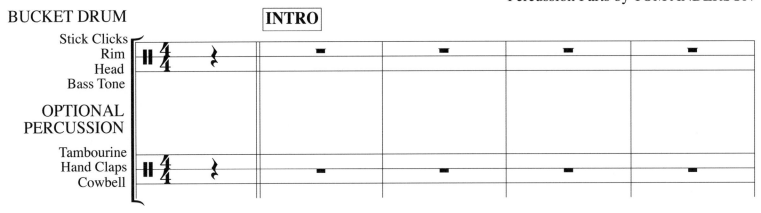

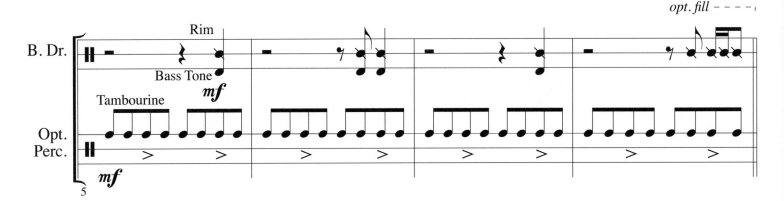

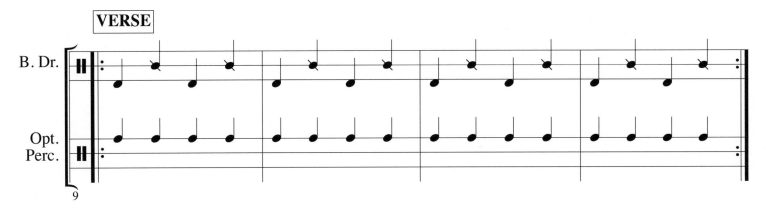

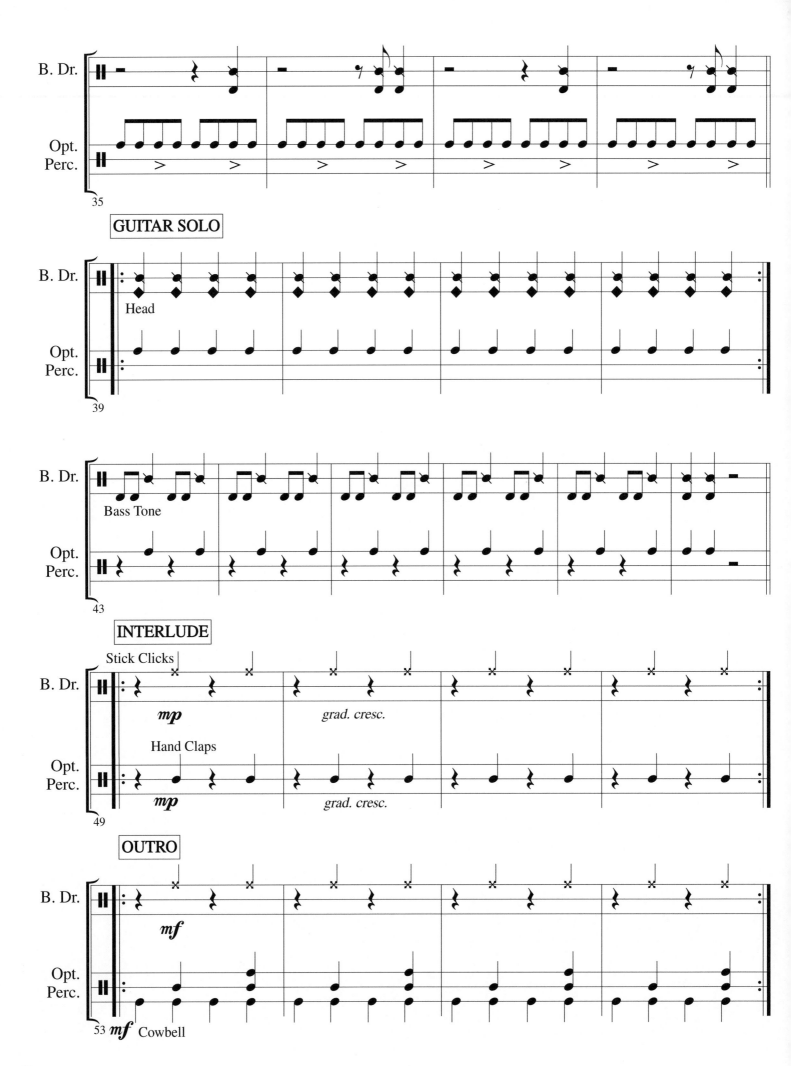

GUITAR SOLO

INTERLUDE

OUTRO

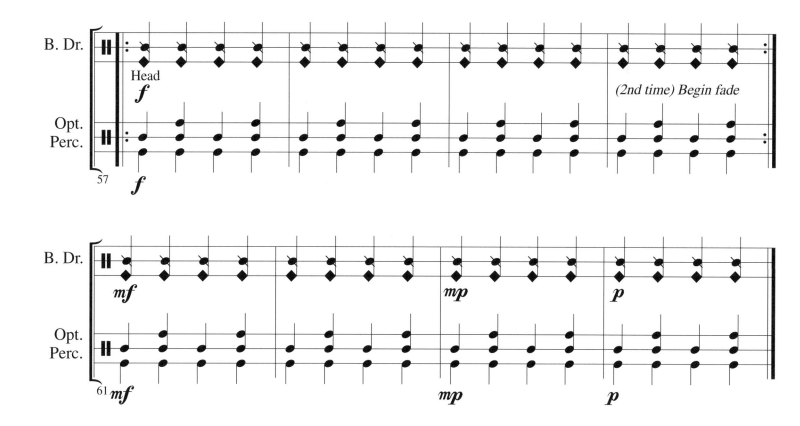

PLAY-ALONG WITH "UPTOWN FUNK"

Teaching Tips by Tom Anderson

BUCKET DRUM WARM-UP 6

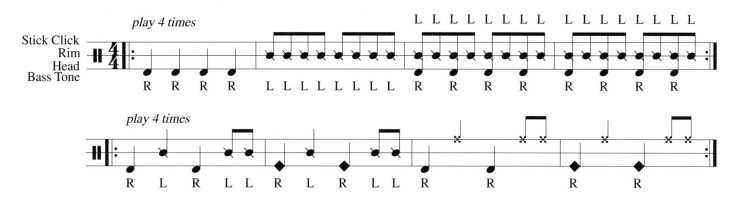

With the infectious underlying rhythm of "boom, bap, boom, bap," it isn't hard to imagine how "Uptown Funk" spent so many weeks at the top of the charts. It was created in a funk jam by the writers. The eventual lead vocalist, Bruno Mars, played the drums. While it is a well-crafted recording, its rhythmic and harmonic simplicity supplies the "hook."

NEW BASS TONE & RIM RHYTHM 1

Most of the bucket drum rhythms have been played in the previous songs. The first new rhythm involves some coordination where the left hand is playing quavers on the rim as the right hand is playing crotchet bass tones.

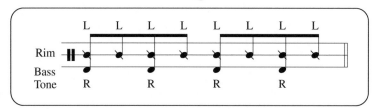

This rhythm is included in Warm-Up 6. A common expectation of drummers is to play two or more rhythms at the same time. With bucket drums, you are using your hands. On a drum kit, you would use your hands <u>and</u> feet.

NEW BASS TONE & RIM RHYTHM 2

Another new rhythm uses these same two tones. Again, the bass tone can be thought of as the bass drum of a drum kit and the rim hit is comparable to a cross stick on the snare drum. This rhythm is also in Warm-Up 6.

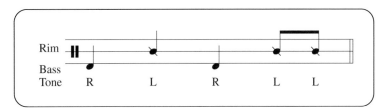

OPTIONAL PERCUSSION

The first **low drum** rhythm fits into the vocal/synthesiser riff at the beginning. Play on beat 1, the "+" of beat 4 and then beat 1; creating a two-bar phrase.

A familiar-sounding **shaker** part is played towards the end of the song. Make sure beats 2 and 4 are accented by moving your hand farther on those beats. Keep the overall quaver feel even; much like the sound of a ticking clock.

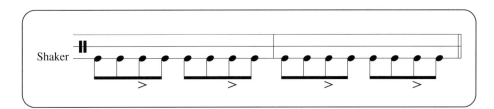

The **hand claps** are on the off beats of 2 & 4.

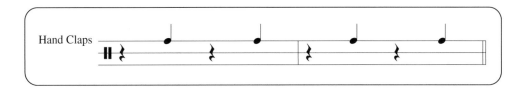

All of the optional percussion instruments are played on the last beat along with a stick click.

PLAY-ALONG WITH "UPTOWN FUNK"

Words and Music by MARK RONSON, BRUNO MARS,
PHILIP LAWRENCE, JEFF BHASKER,
DEVON GALLASPY, NICHOLAUS WILLIAMS,
LONNIE SIMMONS, RONNIE WILSON,
CHARLES WILSON, RUDOLPH TAYLOR
and ROBERT WILSON
Percussion Parts by TOM ANDERSON

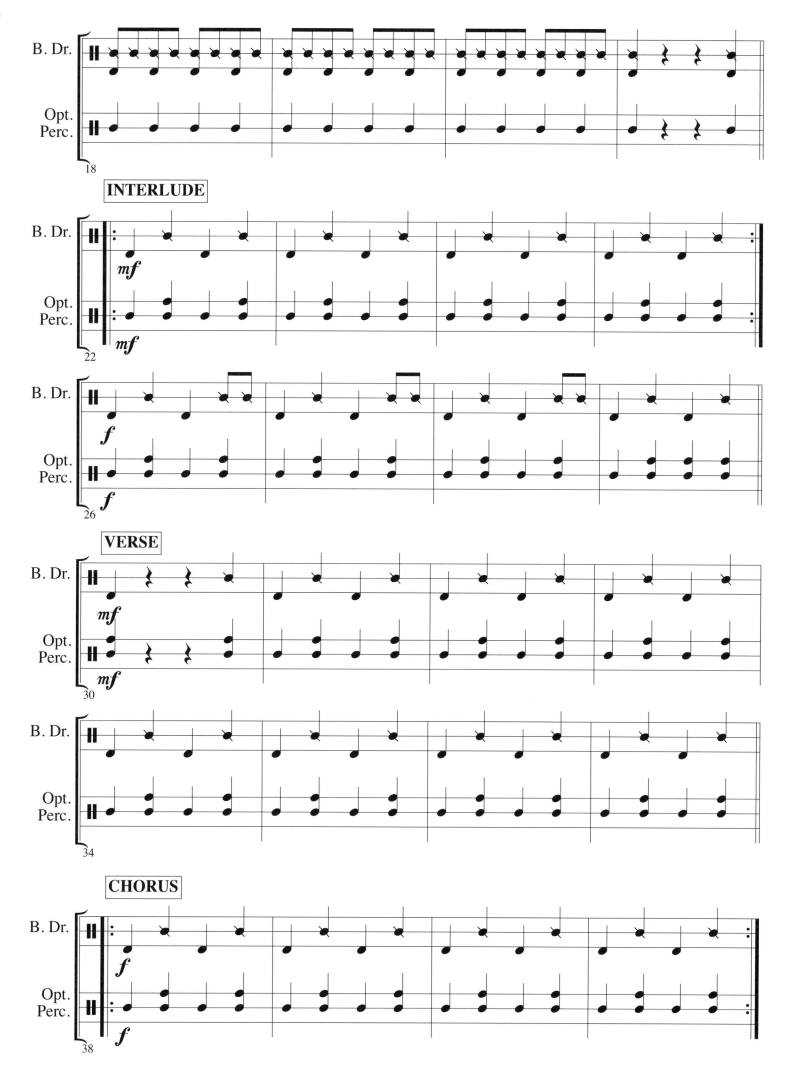

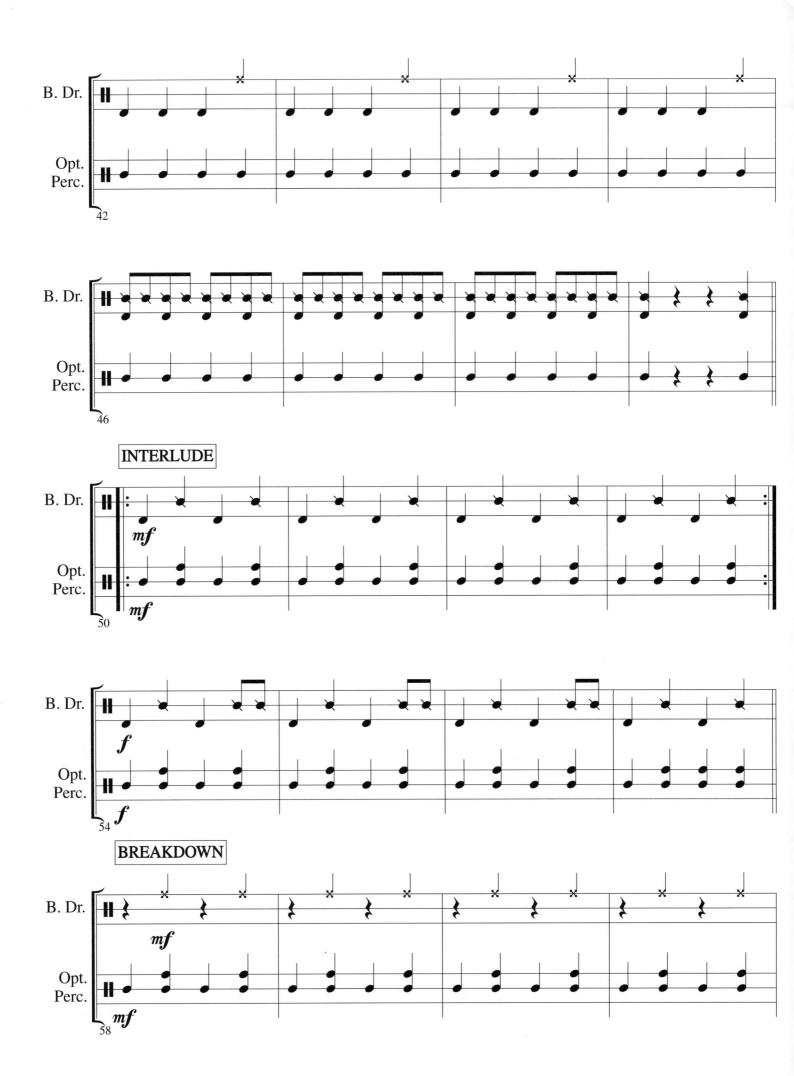

ABOUT THE WRITER
TOM ANDERSON

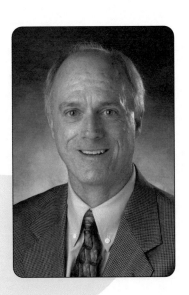

Tom Anderson is a Choral Editor for Hal Leonard Corporation. A music educator for over 20 years, Tom has taught at the kindergarten through university levels in Montana, Colorado, Pennsylvania and Washington state. He holds a Master in Music Education degree from the University of North Texas and a DMA in Choral Conducting from the University of Missouri-Kansas City. Tom sang in the University of North Texas Jazz Singers and studied choral conducting with Eph Ehly and arranging with Kirby Shaw at UMKC. He played guitar in the Bob Curnow Big Band in Spokane, WA. His choral arrangements are published by Hal Leonard as well as classroom resources such as *Music Fact Raps*, *Percussion Cookbook*, *Whacked on Classics*, *Rhythm Read & Play*, *Boomin' the Basics*, and *Rockin' Poppin' Classroom*. Tom is an active musician who plays the piano, drums, bass and guitar.

MORE FOR SCHOOLS FROM HAL LEONARD

HL00359602

Enhance music-making in your school by teaching with *Rhythm Cups*. Using just simple plastic cups and fantastic songs, *Rhythm Cups* will develop performance skills, musical literacy, teamwork and coordination in all children. Learn amazing group rhythmic patterns to perform together, using our easy-to-read rhythm cup notation and popular song collection. Each book comes with a unique code for online access to audio resources and demonstration videos.

Differentiated into simple to more challenging rhythm cup patterns, *Rhythm Cups* is a flexible and affordable resource to engage musical learning across Key Stages 2–3. With no need for a specialist music classroom or expensive resources, this is the ideal musical tool for all primary and KS3 school teachers. Perfect for classroom learning and assemblies!